ideals
VALENTINE

Let this valentine
Be a reminder
That the special love
Which radiates so strongly
At this particular time of year
Is a universal message
Of the everlasting love
That each of us has
To share each and every day.
Love, universal love,
So essential to nurture
Our highest good
Today and forever.

Byron P. Tousignant

ISBN 0-8249-1000-1 350

IDEALS—Vol. 38, No. 1 January MCMLXXXI. IDEALS (ISSN 0019-137X) is published eight times a year,
January, February, April, June, July, September, October, November
by IDEALS PUBLISHING CORPORATION, 11315 Watertown Plank Road, Milwaukee, Wis. 53226
ecònd class postage paid at Milwaukee, Wisconsin. Copyright ® MCMLXXX by IDEALS PUBLISHING CORPORATION.
Postmaster, please send form 3579 to Ideals Publishing Corporation, Post Office Box 2100, Milwaukee, Wis. 53201
All rights reserved. Title IDEALS registered U.S. Patent Office.
Published Simultaneously in Canada.

ONE YEAR SUBSCRIPTION—eight consecutive issues as published—$15.95
TWO YEAR SUBSCRIPTION—sixteen consecutive issues as published—$27.95
SINGLE ISSUE—$3.50

Publisher, James A. Kuse
Managing Editor, Ralph Luedtke
Editor/Ideals, Colleen Callahan Gonring
Associate Editor, Linda Robinson
Production Manager, Mark Brunner
Photographic Editor, Gerald Koser
Copy Editor, Norma Barnes
Art Editor, Duane Weaver

My Treasured Valentine

My heart will always treasure
A favorite valentine,
The one your love has woven
Into golden threads of rhyme.

A dear and precious token
Where beauty leaves its trace,
Where velvet bows of ribbon
Are gleaming in the frilly lace.

My heart will ever cherish
The blue forget-me-nots,
Where lovely wreaths of magic
Twine around your fondest thoughts.

Where hearts and dainty flowers
Weave a memory of gold,
A gift that love has fashioned
With sweetness in each fold.

In all its glowing beauty,
The sweetest, dearest part
Are the little words, "I love you,"
That whisper from your heart.

Joy Belle Burgess

The Basket Social

The kerosene lamps hanging along either wall of the one-room schoolhouse had begun the evening with shining chimneys and well-trimmed wicks. Now it was nearly midnight and they smoked and flickered and were forgotten by the crowd of country people beneath them. The violins had played the last sweet strains of the popular song, "In the Shade of the Old Apple Tree." Some of the dancers were still standing, and an expectant hush pervaded the building.

It was the night of the basket social, an event anticipated by everyone in the community. The girls, from seven to seventy, had been struggling for the past week with paste, shoe boxes and fancy paper, attempting to fashion a basket worthy of the affair. This evening, chicken and ham sandwiches, cake and pie had been stacked into the elaborate and sometimes ludicrous containers and brought to the schoolhouse to be auctioned to the highest bidder. There was a two-fold purpose: to eat supper with one's best beau and at the same time painlessly raise money to buy a new organ for the school.

The auctioner had already mounted the small platform constructed for the event. His assistant, a teenage boy who was grinning sheepishly, now emerged from behind the curtain that screened the baskets. Holding one aloft at a breathtaking angle, he came mincing forward, new shoes squeaking with every step. There was a unanimous sigh of relief as the basket safely reached the capable hands of the auctioneer.

"What am I bid for this work of art?" he boomed in a voice that belied his small stature and thin, stooped shoulders.

Eyes fastened on the basket. Young men nervously wondered if this could be the one their best girl had delicately hinted about. Married men attempted to recognize something familiar in the scraps of obvious wallpaper that decorated it. Then into the vacuum of silence an embarrassed voice piped, "Four bits!"

Necks craned toward the bidder and that individual cleared his throat nervously and turned a deeper crimson. "Four bits . . . four bits . . ." intoned the auctioneer. "Who'll make it a dollar and a half . . . a dollar and a half . . ." Holding the basket close to his long, thin nose, he gave an exaggerated sniff. "I smell chocolate cake!" This raillery brought a sudden titter from the children.

A buxom wife frantically nudged her middle-aged husband until in self-defense, he waved to the auctioneer and shouted, "Me! Me!" The wife, beaming with success, confided in a sibilant whisper to the woman nearest her, "Henry always buys my basket."

Then someone decided Henry should pay more for the privilege, and the bidding grew lively for a moment, then languished. The auctioneer pointed a bony finger at the second bidder and boomed, "Sold to Henry Bayler!" And he grandly added, "This fine gentleman has the honor of making the first deposit toward our new organ!" There was scattered applause. It gave Henry a bit of consolation for the three dollars he had paid to eat his own food.

As each basket was presented there would be murmurs of speculation among the crowd. And if some lad decided it belonged to his girl, the bidding would grow furious and prolonged. Baskets often brought a price that would make a young fellow of the present generation wince. The owner of the sought after basket would blush pink and modestly pretend no interest in the winning bidder. But later on, how she bragged to us girls about the price her beau paid!

I was among the youngest of the young ladies and wearing my hair done up for the first time. I, too, had a basket in pink paper and draped with a string of tinsel borrowed from the Christmas tree ornaments. Every minute of my work on that basket was a dream and a prayer.

But the boy of my dreams never saw the thin, little girl whose angles had not yet grown into curves. He bought a beautiful, white basket trimmed in red, velvet roses. It belonged to the belle of the community.

Hope dies hard. He might yet buy mine, I thought. But that hope was as groundless as my dreams. The auction continued and each time a pink basket appeared, I held my breath and wadded my handkerchief in a tight, moist ball.

Finally the fund for the organ was assured and the auctioneer no longer pleaded and wheedled for the extra four bits. Then that grinning ape of a boy appeared with my basket. I wished he'd fall through the floor and take the basket with him. There was no one left to buy it, no one I cared to eat with! I felt terribly humiliated.

Once more the bidding began. "A dollar and a half!" another bidder offered, "Two!"

"Sold!" shouted the weary auctioneer.

I refused to watch any longer and Mamma prodded me with her elbow. "Elsie, this gentleman has bought your basket."

He was old, even older than Papa. At least forty! Someone introduced him as the man who had recently moved east of the creek. Carrying my basket, he led me toward one of the benches. As we passed, there was a smothered giggle from a group of my girl friends and my face suffused with shame.

A plump, pigeon-like woman smiled a welcome as we approached and made room for us. "I'm Mr. Benson's wife," she chirped. On her lap was a big, granite dishpan filled level with sandwiches. I stared. Sheer consternation forced my stiff lips to exclaim, "Your basket!"

She continued to smile as if it weren't unusual and explained, "I have quite a brood to feed." Brood was the only word to describe them. Children of all sizes clustered around us and the sandwiches began disappearing like magic.

Mr. Benson placed my basket on my lap. He seemed to be waiting. Then I saw him gesture to a tall, brown-eyed boy outside the circle of smaller children. "Here, Son," he called, "is the basket you bid on and the little lady that goes with it."

Once more space was made on the bench and I opened my basket with trembling, inept fingers, scarcely daring to look at my new supper partner. But I was well aware of the envy that had replaced the giggles of my friends.

And just as a basket social sometimes shattered dreams, it could also brew a batch of new ones.

Grace Sellers

Memory

Edna Jaques

Memory wields a tender brush,
Paints the past a lovely shade,
Softens outlines sharp and hard,
Makes the crudest colors fade,
Into a soft blend that seems
Shadowless and dim as dreams.

Memory lays her hands upon
Thoughts of old, remembered strife,
Straightens out the tangled threads
Of the pattern we call life.
How much clearer we can see
Looking back with memory.

Memory gilds the commonplace,
Makes the lonely ways to shine,
Adds a glamor to the days,
Changes that old past of mine
Into something sweet and rare,
Radiant and clean as prayer.

Memory is a school where we
Learn that only good can be
Carried down across the years,
Time's eternal tapestry.
Living colors rich and rare
Woven in a pattern there.

Valentine's Day

So many fanciful, romantic tales surround the history of Valentine's Day that we sophisticated moderns may have come to treat it too lightly. Whether the origin is to be found in the Roman Feast of the Lupercalia or in the generous soul of St. Valentine, who secretly placed food on the doorstep of the worthy poor, the motif is the finest type of kindness. The nucleus of all celebration of the day is an anonymous gesture of friendship. Doing something for someone without hope of reward is a noble act. It is a human characteristic to want recognition and reward. Only those whose generosity prompts them to give of their worldly goods or their time or their talents anonymously know what supreme personal happiness and spiritual compensation one receives from such service.

Author Unknown

Friends

The friends upon my windowsill
Are gay all winter long
With blooms of purple, pink, and red
That thrive through wintry storms.

My friends are regal violets
And bright geraniums,
Azaleas and cactus plants
And gold chrysanthemums.

They greet each visitor to our home
In quite a special way,
Their friendly blossoms pressed up close
Against the windowpane.

They ask so little for themselves
And give such splendor rare
That I have come to treasure them
As friends for whom I care.

Craig E. Sathoff

"I Do Solemnly Swear . . ."

Bea Bourgeois

They have been occasions of triumph and tragedy, of great joy and nearly unspeakable sorrow; they have been both festive and funereal. Since the very first Inauguration Day, when George Washington was sworn into office on April 30, 1789, American Presidents have begun their terms in office under circumstances as volatile as history itself.

Because the Supreme Court was not yet in existence at the time of Washington's first Inaugural, the oath of office was administered, in New York City, by Robert R. Livingston, Chancellor of the State of New York. It was the first time that the formal promise was heard in the land: "I do solemnly swear that I will faithfully execute the office of the President of the United States, and will, to the best of my ability, preserve, protect and defend the Constitution of the United States."

Ceremonies surrounding Inauguration Day have ranged from the utterly simple to the wildly flamboyant. Thomas Jefferson's two Inaugurals reflected his "Republican simplicity"; on the first occasion—March 4, 1801—he walked from his home to the Capitol; on the second—March 4, 1805—he rode alone on horseback. John Adams, bitterly disappointed at Jefferson's election in 1800 and chafing at his own loss of the Presidency, refused to accompany Jefferson to the first Inaugural; instead, Adams quietly left Washington without even putting in an appearance.

Jefferson's two Inaugurals reflected his own austerity, but one of the biggest parties in the land followed the Inauguration of James Buchanan on March 4, 1857. The ceremony was followed by a ball, attended by about six thousand merrymakers, and a banquet of staggering proportions. Guests managed to consume hundreds of gallons of oysters and chicken salad, ice cream and jellies, along with sixty saddles of mutton, eight rounds of beef, and seventy-five hams.

Several Inauguration Days have come as a shock to men who never thought they would be sitting in the White House. William Henry Harrison was a war hero who won the Presidency in 1840 and had chosen John Tyler as his running mate. Tyler never dreamed he would become President, but fate intervened; Harrison's own Inauguration Day proved to be fatal to his health.

After reading the longest Inaugural speech in the history of the country, Harrison rode his horse in the parade and joined the nonstop festivities by dancing at three separate balls. Despite the severe weather, Harrison refused to ride in a covered carriage and braved the elements on horseback.

The cold rain during the Inaugural parade and the exhaustion that Harrison experienced after the ceremonies conspired to produce a chill that led to the illness which killed him on April 4, 1841. The stunned Tyler was sworn in on April 6.

James A. Garfield had reluctantly accepted the Republican nomination for President in 1880 and had chosen Chester A. Arthur as Vice-President. Garfield began his term of office March 4, 1881; on September 2, it was announced that Garfield would leave Washington by train for a New England vacation.

Among the crowd of people at the station waiting to see the President was Charles Julius Guiteau, a religious fanatic who had decided that Garfield was the personification of evil and that God had chosen Guiteau to kill the President.

As the Presidential party walked toward the platform, Guiteau fired a shot that entered Garfield's back, and another that went through his arm. The President lived until September 19; on that day, Chester Alan Arthur became, to his great surprise, the twenty-first President of the United States.

The death of Franklin Delano Roosevelt on April 12, 1945, brought his Vice-President, Harry S. Truman, to the Presidency. Truman, summoned to the White House late in the afternoon, did not know the nature of the call. He was greeted by Eleanor Roosevelt with the words, "Harry, the President is dead."

Truman's Inauguration that day took place in the Cabinet Room of the White House. Chief Justice Harlan F. Stone administered the oath of office, and at nine minutes after seven, Harry Truman had become President of the United States.

Perhaps the shortest—yet most poignant—Inauguration Address was delivered by Lyndon Baines Johnson on November 22, 1963. President John F. Kennedy had been assassinated in Dallas, Texas; the country and the world were in a state of shock and confusion. Johnson realized that several hours would elapse before he could return to Washington, and that the country would be in a vulnerable position without a Chief Executive. Mrs. Sarah T. Hughes, recently appointed a Federal District judge, was summoned aboard Air Force Number One to administer the oath of office to Lyndon Johnson.

Johnson's first Inaugural address reflected the piercing grief of a stunned nation: "This is a sad time for all people. We have suffered a loss that cannot be weighed. For me, it is a deep personal tragedy. I know the world shares the sorrow that Mrs. Kennedy and her family

bear. I will do my best. That is all I can do. I ask for your help—and God's."

Following the official ceremonies that marked their Inaugurations, each of the thirty-eight Presidents has left his singular mark on the highest office in the land. Few of them, however, have had anything good to say about the Presidency.

Thomas Jefferson commented, "Never did a prisoner released from his chains feel such relief as I shall on shaking off the shackles of power." Truman remarked that "Being a President is like riding a tiger. A man has to keep riding or be swallowed." And in September, 1899, William McKinley said of the Presidency, "I have had enough of it, heaven knows! I have had all the honor there is in this place, and have had responsibilities enough to kill any man."

A Valentine Wish

A valentine of hearts and lace
 Came just for me today,
Complete with the inscription,
 "Dad, you're great in every way."

I smiled to see the signature,
 My son's name written bold,
For he was such a little boy,
 Just barely three-months old.

My wife had spoken from her heart
 The wishes sent to me
And loaned them to my infant son
 With all sincerity.

They served to thrill me deep within
 And make me vow to be
The kind of dad who fills the words
 The greeting gave to me.

The deepest wish that I will hold
 Is that I'll hear him say
In ten or fifteen years from now,
 "You're great in every way."
                    Craig E. Sathoff

Frozen Fruits . . . A Taste of Summer

A taste of summer in the heart of winter can take the chill off the season. The fresh, ripe fruits and berries you put in the freezer last summer are sure to bring a special flavor and brightness to your winter table. Most frozen fruit can be used in as many delicious ways as fresh fruit.

For best results, thaw fruits in their original freezing containers, rotating containers during thawing to keep fruit moistened with juice. At room temperature, allow two to three hours for one-pound packages. Refrigerator thawing will take several times longer. To thaw more quickly, place fruit containers in cool running water. Do not refreeze thawed fruit. Leftover fruit should be used in some cooked form, such as a sauce or dessert.

Enjoy the refreshing taste of last summer's fruit . . . this winter! Serve fruit alone, with ice cream, or use in salads, pies, cakes, cobblers and other desserts. These recipes are sure to send you running to the freezer . . . right now!

RHUBARB CRISP

    4 c. sliced rhubarb
    ½ c. butter
    ¾ c. brown sugar, firmly packed
    ½ c. all-purpose flour
    ½ t. cinnamon
    1 c. oatmeal

Arrange rhubarb in shallow baking dish. Cream butter; blend in sugar, flour, and cinnamon. Stir in oatmeal. Sprinkle mixture over rhubarb. Bake in preheated 375° oven 25 to 30 minutes. Serve warm. Serves 6.

NOTE: Lemon juice may be sprinkled over rhubarb for added tartness.

PEACH CHEESECAKE

    1 c. flour
    1 small pkg. vanilla pudding
    1 egg
    ½ c. milk
    1 t. baking powder
    16 ozs. frozen peaches, thawed
       and drained, reserving juice
    1 8-oz. pkg. cream cheese, softened
    ½ c. sugar
    2 T. sugar
    ½ t. cinnamon

Combine first 5 ingredients in a small mixing bowl. Beat for 2 minutes. Pour into a greased 9-inch pie plate or springform. Place peaches over top of batter. Combine cream cheese, ½ cup sugar and 3 tablespoons reserved juice in a small bowl and beat until smooth and creamy. Spread over top of peaches to within ½-inch of the outside edge. Combine the 2 tablespoons sugar and cinnamon. Sprinkle over top of the cheese. Bake at 350° for 40 minutes or until crust is completely baked. Serves 6 to 8.

FRUIT SALAD

    3 to 4 c. mixed frozen fruit, such as
       peaches, strawberries or blueberries,
       thawed and drained
    1 banana, sliced
    1 small can chunk pineapple, drained,
       optional
    1 small pkg. instant vanilla pudding
    1 c. milk
    2 T. orange juice
    3 c. frozen non-dairy whipped topping,
       thawed

Combine frozen fruit, banana and pineapple in a salad bowl, reserving ½ cup. Place pudding, milk and orange juice in a small mixing bowl and beat for 2 minutes. Gradually add whipped topping, beating until creamy and smooth. Pour pudding mixture over fruit and top with reserved fruit. Serves 4 to 6.

Crystal Beauty

The golden sun was shining
    Upon a world of ice;
And for that crystal beauty
    There was no offered price.

The trees encased in silver,
    And some with golden hue,
Stood etched in brilliant diamonds
    Against the sky of blue.

The fields, the lawns, the meadows,
    The hedge and fencetops, too,
Were all a frozen picture—
    Of what God's hands could do.

Gertrude Rudberg

Winter White

Softly, silently, the snowflakes fall,
And flannel-posted fences raise their heads
Along the winding miles of ermine shrubs,
Down roadsides lined with crystal flower beds.
The intricate design of frosted lakes
Gleams dully neath a matted sky of gray,
Pale pointed fingers of the north wind tear
The frozen branches roughly from its way.
Like a scene within a water globe,
The smallest hand need only shake to see
The dazzling swirl that breathlessly descends,
To shape and shade in fragile mystery . . .
So the world appears to me tonight,
Dressed in flowing robes of WINTER WHITE!

Grace E. Easley

Pototschnik © '80

Valentine's Day Story
Keith Havens

Todd lived with his father and mother and two younger sisters in the little town of Winslow during the Great Depression. He was a good-looking boy of seven years, who liked to tell everyone he was almost eight. And he would be, too, next September!

His father was a carpenter who, like many others back in those times, was out of work. But his mother managed to keep food on the table by earning a little money sewing for some of their neighbors.

Now, it was almost Valentine's Day, and Todd had a big problem of his own. He was determined to get the biggest and most beautiful valentine in town to give to Jennifer, the lovely little golden-haired girl who lived across the street. Oh, how he longed to see her smiling face and sparkling blue eyes as she tore away the envelope to see his big surprise! But where would he get the money to buy such a big, beautiful valentine?

He dared not ask his mother for money. He knew she needed every cent just to feed the family. His dad's pockets were empty, and Todd himself had spent the last of his own meager savings at Christmastime.

Todd wandered down the street with his little dog, Sparky. Brooding about his great dilemma and poking aimlessly at the snow with a stick, he thought to himself, "Maybe I could earn some money chopping wood for Mr. Johnson the way I did last fall!"

He hurried along now. Mr. Johnson's house was just down the block. Todd's feet stopped their steady gait as he reached Mr. Johnson's house and peered over the fence into the backyard. His heart sank as he looked at the towering wood pile neatly nestled beneath the eaves of the house. With that dream shattered, Todd looked down at Sparky and said, hopefully, "Well, maybe it will snow some more and then I can get a job shoveling!" Sparky lifted an ear, yipped a couple of times, and then they both went off toward home.

Todd went to bed that evening feeling mighty low. He knew Valentine's Day was only two days away! Just what could he do?

In the morning he awoke to the most beautiful sight his eyes could possibly have beheld! Six full inches of new snow had fallen overnight! It didn't take Todd long to eat a quick breakfast, grab his shovel, and be off down the block, with Sparky following!

By mid-afternoon Todd had shoveled the Peabody's walk and long driveway. Then, for good measure, he had shoveled the walk and steps of old Mrs. Trittlewitz, who lived all alone. Now, with his hard-earned money burning a hole in his pocket, Todd raced down the street with Sparky. He headed toward the big drugstore in the main corner of town. He knew they had lots of greeting cards and big, beautiful valentines!

Sparky had to wait outside the store while his master went in to look for the biggest, most beautiful valentine he could possibly imagine! Suddenly, there it was, just jumping out at Todd! He took the card to the counter to pay for it, but the clerk told him he didn't have enough money to pay for *that* big a valentine! As Todd slowly walked out of the store, looking longingly back over his shoulder at the big display of valentines, a big tear rolled down his rosy cheek.

On their way home Todd and Sparky walked past Jennifer's house, and Todd saw her through the window as she sat at the piano practicing her lesson. He had a vision of her hugging him and kissing his cheek as she opened the valentine he could not afford to buy! Tears came to his eyes again and he turned and quickly walked across the street to his house.

Then, as Todd saw his own footprints in the snow, suddenly a light seemed to go on in his head! He knew right then that as surely as tomorrow was Valentine's Day, Jennifer *would* have the biggest, most beautiful valentine she had ever seen!

With lightning speed, Todd ran to the grocery store and bought as much bright red vegetable dye as his snow-shoveling money could purchase! Then he ran right back to Jennifer's house. There, in the dim evening light of the street lamp, and right underneath her window, Todd tramped down the glistening snow and designed the biggest and most beautiful valentine in the whole world! Right in Jennifer's front yard!

There was one huge red heart right in the middle all colored with red vegetable dye! And then Todd took a stick and wrote the words "BE MY VALENTINE" in the snow under the heart!

The very next morning, when Jennifer greeted the sun shining through her window, she saw the biggest, most beautiful valentine she had ever seen in all her life trampled in the snow right outside her window! Her blue eyes sparkled as she grabbed her coat and ran out of the house to follow the footprints in the snow, which led across the street to Todd's house.

"Todd," she said, "Dear Todd! Your valentine is the most beautiful I've ever seen!" And she hugged him and kissed his cheek! And Todd's face got all flushed, and Sparky put a paw over one of his ears because he was happy, too!

To My
Dear and Loving
Husband

If ever two were one, then surely we.
If ever man were loved by wife, then thee.

If ever wife was happy in a man.
Compare with me, ye women, if you can.

I prize thy love more than whole mines of gold,
Or all the riches that the East doth hold.

My love is such that rivers cannot quench,
Nor ought but love from thee give recompense.

Thy love is such I can no way repay;
The heavens reward thee manifold I pray.

Then while we live, in love let's so persevere,
That when we live no more, we may live ever.

Anne Bradstreet

Living Lace ❧ *From Nature*

Ferns are the living laces that add elegance to every community in which they grow and complement every plant with which they are associated. The graceful fronds (the leaves) are usually highly divided to produce a delicate pattern that subtly pleases the eye and greatly enhances the surrounding environment. Since ancient times, these graceful patterns have been admired, inspiring their use in our arts and crafts to increase the beauty of the nonliving world.

Such grace and distinction should not be neglected in our own indoor and outdoor living areas. There are ferns for every situation, from sun to deep shade, from dry to very wet soils, from sand and rocks to rich humus. Despite a rugged climate that varies from Arctic winter to tropical summer, Wisconsin has about ninety species of ferns. This number increases rapidly as one goes east or south or into mountain areas. Ferns are found in open fields, in the shade of deep woods, clinging to cracks and crevices of deep cliffs and rock ledges, and decorating water edges and other wetland communities.

Since early times, the fern family has continually diminished as the climate has changed and the earth has been increasingly disturbed by construction, agriculture, lumbering, drainage, and waste disposal. In recent times, ferns generally have been ignored as people have sought the more obviously beautiful flowering plants. Our elegant ferns deserve a better fate.

Many ferns thrive under conditions which limit the growth of flowering plants. Places too shady for grasses can support a large variety of attractive ferns; such places include areas along the north side of a home or garage, between closely spaced buildings, within courtyards of homes and businesses, in shaded nooks and crannies of the porch or veranda, and under trees and shrubs.

Among the species excellent for these shaded areas are the dainty and distinctive Maidenhair Fern (*Adriantum datum*), six to fifteen inches high, that thrives in rich, moist soil out of the wind; the aptly named Florist Fern or Spiny Wood Fern (*Dryopteris spenulosa* and varieties), twelve to twenty-four inches high, with an attractive, finely divided rosette of fronds, thriving in the damp soil of woods, among rocks, and clinging to crumbling logs; the graceful and finely divided Lady Fern (*Athyrium filix-mina*), one and one-half to three feet high, which grows readily, even in the sun if the soil remains moist; the dusky, attractive Cinnamon Fern (*Osmunda cinnamonia*), two to five feet high, for rich, moist soil in sun or shade, forming an excellent background; the quite similarly attractive Interrupted Fern (*Osmunda claytomiana*), one and one-half to four feet high, which tolerates both swamp edges and dry shady sites; the large majestic Ostrich Fern

(*Pteretis modulosa*), two to five feet high, that loves the moist, rich soil; and lastly, one of the most attractive, the Goldies Fern (*Dryopteris goldiana*), two and one-half to four feet high, with graceful, luxurious fronds, easily grown in rich, moist soil.

Those who have either natural or developed rock gardens, rock ledges or rock walls will be delighted with a number of excellent ferns that grow in cracks and crevices of rocks and in rocky areas. These include the delicate Maidenhair Spleenwort (*Asplenium trichomanes*), two to ten inches high, which is very desirable in shady rock gardens; the Bulblet Fern (*Cystopteris bulbifera*), six to twenty inches high, which grows best in shady limestone pockets and crevices in moist soil; the very attractive little Fragile Fern (*Cystopteris fragilis*), three to twelve inches, that is easily grown in shady rock areas; the desirable small Oak Fern (*Dryopteris disjuncta*), four to sixteen inches high, for the shaded rock garden or nook; the attractive Florist or Spiny Wood Fern, previously listed; the small Purple Cliff-brake Fern (*Pellae atropurpurea*), three to twelve inches, for exposed calcareous rocks, walls and cliffs; the pleasing Common Polypody, previously listed, for shady, rich rock gardens and banks; the excellent Rusty Woodsia, previously listed, that endures sun or shade among rocks and on rock ledges; and the delicately laced Blunt-lobed Woodsia (*Woodsia obtusa*), ten to eighteen inches high, for shady ledges and rocky woods.

As indoor gardening becomes increasingly popular, ferns are being more extensively used as room decorations. Unfortunately, the dry winter air of many homes makes fern survival difficult. The problem is compounded if any remnant of stove gas escapes into the air. An easy way to grow ferns successfully indoors is to use terrariums or similar enclosed areas in which moist air can be maintained. With a favorable environment, several native ferns can be grown indoors, including the excellent Ebony Spleenwort (*Asplenium platyneuron*), six to sixteen inches high; and four previously mentioned—the lacy Bulblet Fern, which multiplies readily; the attractive Common Polypody; the handsome Marginal Shield Fern; and the Christmas Fern, which resembles the Boston Fern. As they multiply, some ferns can be planted outdoors during warmer weather, decorating both indoor and backyard gardens.

The dainty elegance of the ferns combined with their unique hardiness in less favorable environmental conditions recommend them for wider use in both formal and naturalized areas. They can be used as specimen plants, as background material, or in combination with garden flowers or wild flowers. They are exceptionally good for complementing other plants and adding a plush appearance to entire borders.

Valentine Greetings
From Sub-zero Freeze
to Subtropic Breeze

Greetings from the sunny south!

Is this really winter? If it is, then I must be dreaming. What a way to spend the winter! For putting roses in my cheeks, I much prefer skimming across foamy waves to skiing down slippery slopes; water stings less in liquid form.

Lounging on a warm, sandy beach shaded by towering palms, I have trouble visualizing the rest of the continent still wrapped in winter's icy grip. It is quite possible that I have become afflicted with one of two maladies common to this region of the country: either the continuous Florida sunshine has warped my perspective of seasons, or I am undergoing a mild case of self-inflicted amnesia. I am reasonably certain, however, that as soon as my last week of vacation dissolves, any such ailments will rapidly follow suit.

Yesterday we went deep-sea fishing. Of course, we didn't hook any fish (nothing new about that), but we did catch—on film—a remarkable assortment of sea life ranging from manta rays to sharks to goldfish. Although such creatures are fascinating, I hope never to see the likes of them swimming in Lake Michigan.

Tomorrow we begin our tour of the sites in and around Orlando. We've been assured that would be at least a three-day accomplishment. In addition to the amusement parks, gardens and other points of interest, we hope to squeeze in a few rounds of golf somewhere. I could stay in this subtropic paradise forever!

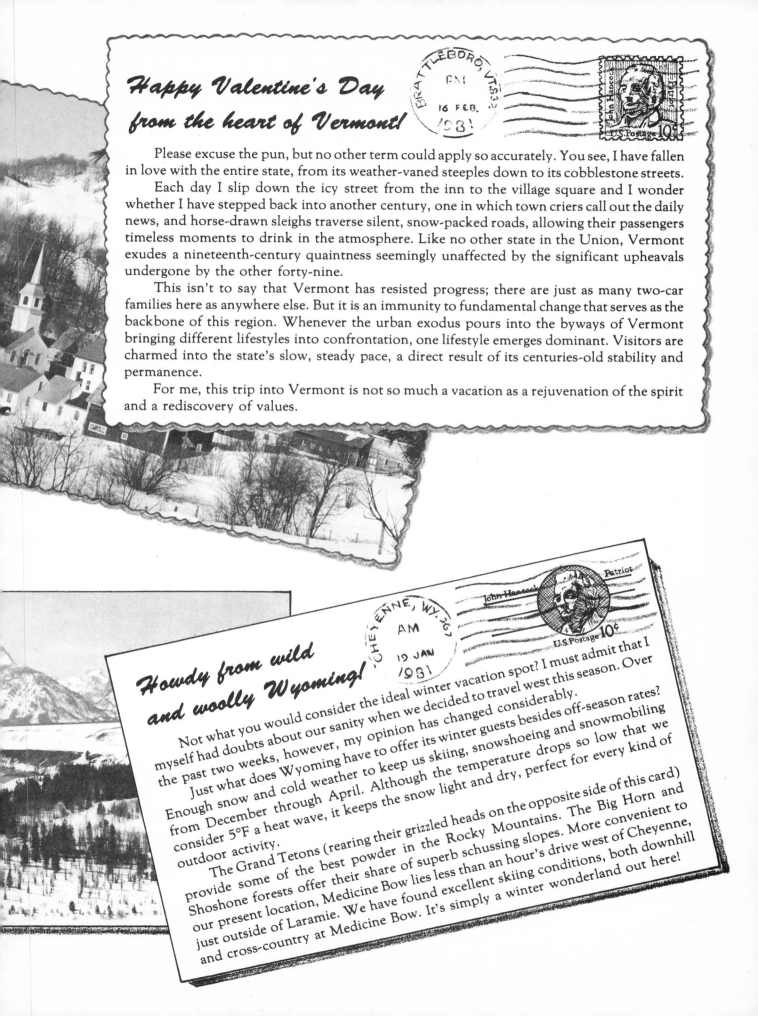

Happy Valentine's Day from the heart of Vermont!

Please excuse the pun, but no other term could apply so accurately. You see, I have fallen in love with the entire state, from its weather-vaned steeples down to its cobblestone streets.

Each day I slip down the icy street from the inn to the village square and I wonder whether I have stepped back into another century, one in which town criers call out the daily news, and horse-drawn sleighs traverse silent, snow-packed roads, allowing their passengers timeless moments to drink in the atmosphere. Like no other state in the Union, Vermont exudes a nineteenth-century quaintness seemingly unaffected by the significant upheavals undergone by the other forty-nine.

This isn't to say that Vermont has resisted progress; there are just as many two-car families here as anywhere else. But it is an immunity to fundamental change that serves as the backbone of this region. Whenever the urban exodus pours into the byways of Vermont bringing different lifestyles into confrontation, one lifestyle emerges dominant. Visitors are charmed into the state's slow, steady pace, a direct result of its centuries-old stability and permanence.

For me, this trip into Vermont is not so much a vacation as a rejuvenation of the spirit and a rediscovery of values.

Howdy from wild and woolly Wyoming!

Not what you would consider the ideal winter vacation spot? I must admit that I myself had doubts about our sanity when we decided to travel west this season. Over the past two weeks, however, my opinion has changed considerably.

Just what does Wyoming have to offer its winter guests besides off-season rates? Enough snow and cold weather to keep us skiing, snowshoeing and snowmobiling from December through April. Although the temperature drops so low that we consider 5°F a heat wave, it keeps the snow light and dry, perfect for every kind of outdoor activity.

The Grand Tetons (rearing their grizzled heads on the opposite side of this card) provide some of the best powder in the Rocky Mountains. The Big Horn and Shoshone forests offer their share of superb schussing slopes. More convenient to our present location, Medicine Bow lies less than an hour's drive west of Cheyenne, just outside of Laramie. We have found excellent skiing conditions, both downhill and cross-country at Medicine Bow. It's simply a winter wonderland out here!

Remembering

Memories are treasured things
That keep the heart aglow,
Linking years with yesteryears
And loves we used to know.

Memories are links of gold
Connecting old and new,
The dearest recollections
Of things we used to do.

Memories are treasured bits
With dream-thoughts most sublime,
Reweaving life's true journey
To join the hand of time.

Mamie Ozburn Odum

Black-capped Chickadee

Donald W. Stokes and Deborah Prince

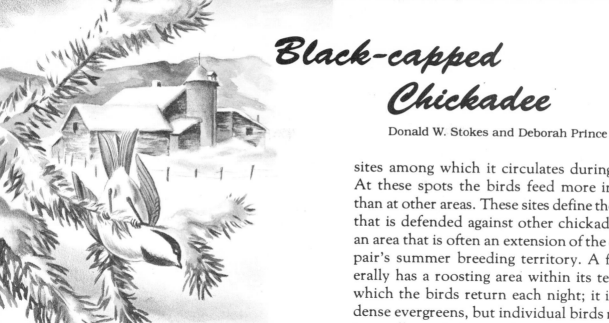

Chickadees are some of the best birds to study in winter. They have interesting behavior and are present all winter in noisy and conspicuous flocks. However, these flocks are not like the loose-knit, free-roaming winter flocks of other birds; they are stable in membership and have rigid social structure. The flocks average six birds and form around a dominant pair which bred the previous summer. Other members may be juveniles that may or may not be the young of the dominant pair, as well as a few stray adults. While watching the flock you may see one bird usurp another's feeding perch by scaring it away. This is a common expression of dominance among birds, and in this case it is an expression of the hierarchical structure of the flock.

When out walking you may repeatedly find a chickadee flock in the same place. This is because a flock will have three to five favorite foraging sites among which it circulates during the day. At these spots the birds feed more intensively than at other areas. These sites define the territory that is defended against other chickadee flocks, an area that is often an extension of the dominant pair's summer breeding territory. A flock generally has a roosting area within its territory to which the birds return each night; it is often in dense evergreens, but individual birds may roost in small tree holes nearby.

Chickadees have a number of calls which make them easy to locate in the woods. Each call is more or less associated with a certain function. Their most frequent call is their "contact note." This is a high-pitched "tseet-tseet" and is continually given by members of the flock in order to keep the flock together. When a bird has strayed farther away it may give the well-known call "chickadee-dee" to locate the flock. A scolding call is given to express dominance within the flock or between flocks; it is just "dee-dee-dee-dee," and is often given when a dominant bird is displacing another from a feeding perch.

The chickadee has an extraordinary ability to maneuver on branches. It is as comfortable hanging below as it is perching on top. In winter, half of its diet is small eggs or larvae of insects and spiders which are nestled in bark crevices. The rest consists of seeds from pines and hemlocks. It has been suggested that the chickadee's acrobatic ability is an adaptation to winter feeding —when snow covers the tops of evergreen branches, chickadees can still hang beneath to gather seeds and insects.

In September and October local flocks of chickadees are augmented by migrant chickadee flocks. But by November only a few are left, and you have to travel over a number of woodland acres to see or hear a flock. But at this time the flocks begin to be joined by other species, such as nuthatches, woodpeckers, kinglets, brown creepers, and titmice. These are only loose associations, with each species coming and going at different times of day.

Excerpt from *A Guide to Nature in Winter: Northeast and North-Central North America* by Donald W. Stokes and Deborah Prince. Copyright © 1976 by Donald W. Stokes and Deborah Prince. By permission of Little, Brown and Company.

Let me paint a snowdrift country
On a lovely winter's day;
Let me mix and match the colors
Of white, blue-white, and gray.

Let me grasp the icy fingers
Of this sprite they call Jack Frost,
And dip my brush in golden sun,
Faint . . . but not yet lost.

Let me toss the silver of a star
To give the blue-black heavens light . . .
To finish . . . let me frame my canvas
In the windless peace of night.

Let me catch the flash of crimson
Of skiers on a snowy slope;
Let me capture the easy rhythm
Of a skater's grace and scope.

Winterscape

Lois J. Martinec

February, with its brief thaw, brings a change in the air at Stillmeadow. More winter's ahead, but now I go out to cut branches of pussy willow to bring indoors to bloom.

Butternut Wisdom

Gladys Taber

The color of February is slate, with low scudding clouds in an opaque sky. Wet snow falls on my meadow, and the yard is slippery with ice. The main topic of conversation in the village is whether this, or March, is the worst month in New England. Weather, of course, is always a major subject, as most of us live on scattered farms, and transportation is by car—equipped with snow tires and maybe chains.

But February is short, and somewhere in the middle comes the blessed February thaw. Out comes a happy sun, snow melts, skies are sapphire, and the air smells of damp woods and thawing brooks. It smells of the spring to come—that is how it smells—and I go out with the Irish and the cocker and gulp the air until I am dizzy.

I wonder sometimes if we do not need in our lives a February as well as May. Anyway, New Englanders are accustomed to the changing seasons, and I think they're lost when they go to kinder climates.

This is the time homemakers begin to think of spring cleaning (it is much too early) and planting gardens (a long way off) and putting on that new roof (no man will climb to a ridgepole while it is snowing and freezing). But somehow the February thaw turns the heart toward April and the first violets. The heart has its own seasons.

By now my woodpile diminishes, but Joe tells me it will last another winter. He cuts the wood on my own land, as trees fall. Since I hate waste, this gives me a warm feeling. I am sad when I drive around the countryside and see dead timber rotting on abandoned farm lands. We are a wasteful country, as the dreadful water shortages of past summers attest. We root up forests, drain marshes, dam up streams, and then wonder why there isn't enough water. Nature, in her quiet, remorseless way, repays us for ignoring her laws.

Valentine day is a lovely holiday and entirely suits my romantic nature. My feeling, as I have said before, is that if you want to send funny valentines, forget the whole thing. This day is for roses and violets and pink frosting on cakes and a chance to say "I love you" without seeming too emotional. We are a reserved people, for the most part, and I wish we could more often tell those we love how we feel. As for me, I begin every day by telling Holly I couldn't love her more than yesterday, but I just do. I tell my dear ones as often as I dare how much they mean to me, too.

I have some friends who spend most of their time reprimanding their dogs for various faults, scolding them for inconsequentials. I notice they complain to me that their dogs are nervous and jumpy and unmanageable. Which makes me wonder if one reason all of my dogs have been merry and gentle and obedient is because they have been told daily how special and wonderful they are.

This applies even more to children. When I meet a child, I always know just how the parents have treated that child from the beginning. Love is the priceless ingredient in life.

Gladys Taber

Gladys Taber, well-known author and columnist, left behind volumes of poetry, novels, plays and other works, mostly chronicling country life in New England, before her recent death on March 11, 1980, at age eighty. She was born in Colorado Springs, Colorado, in 1899 and spent most of her youth moving about the country, due to her father's occupation as a mining engineer. Her summers, however, were usually spent on her grandfather's farm in Massachusetts. Eventually, her family settled in Wisconsin, where her father became the head of the Geology Department at Lawrence College. Mrs. Taber received a B.A. degree from Wellesley College in 1920 and an M.A. degree in 1921 from Lawrence University. She taught English at various colleges before embarking on a professional writing career in 1932. Many readers of the *Ladies Home Journal* and *Family Circle* magazine are familiar with Mrs. Taber's columns, which appeared regularly in those magazines for years. Gladys Taber remains best remembered for her nonfiction books based on her experiences in rural life at Stillmeadow, a seventeenth century farmhouse in Southbury, Connecticut, and at Still Cove, a small house overlooking Mill Pond in Orleans, Massachusetts. Her better known works include *Mrs. Daffodil, Another Path, The Stillmeadow Road, Country Chronicles, Amber—A Very Personal Cat,* and *My Own Cape Cod.*

Fairy Frost

Sometime between the dusk and dawn,
    A mystic blanket fell,
And made the old earth like some place
    Where only fairies dwell.
Each tree seemed dipped in festive frost,
    With glimmering jewels fraught,
And magic on each bare, plain twig
    Festoons of silver wrought.

Each bush was changed from dull, dead brown
    To glistening, gleaming white,
As fair as summer's fresh, fair green
    And blue, and rose, and white.
All through the air there seemed a mist
    Of diamond dust so fine,
Till every bush and branch and limb
    In radiance seemed to shine.

Each tinseled shrub and vine drooped down,
    With fairy jewels bent;
Against the azure of the sky
    Their shining brightness blent;
And slowly yielding to the rays
    That shone in brightness down,
The fairyland soon disappeared—
    The trees were bare and brown.

Hazel Adell Jackson

Dan A. Hoover

Widely known for his poetry and nature stories, the late Dan A. Hoover of Hillsboro, Illinois, was driven by the need to express himself. Born to a poor Illinois farm family in 1906, Hoover completed high school and educated himself to write. He started with short stories, then turned to writing nature research articles and poetry for such publications as *Ranger Rick's Nature Magazine, Jack and Jill, Illinois Wildlife, Golden Magazine, The Living Wilderness, Ideals,* and many others. Mr. Hoover's interest in children and nature has inspired the creation of a great nature program for the Texas elementary school which his granddaughter attends. The staff and over seven hundred students of Oak Creek Elementary School recently dedicated the Dan A. Hoover Memorial Nature Library, in memory of the Illinois author. The establishment of a nature library furthers Dan Hoover's life-long goal to enrich the lives of children by cultivating an awareness of and an appreciation for nature. In addition to writing poetry, Mr. Hoover was an amateur radio enthusiast, along with his wife and two children. Employed by the Illinois Power Company for forty-four years, he worked his way up from an office boy to an electrical engineer. His life story and poetry remain an inspiration to us all.

Eternal Valentine

Did you know each passing minute
Makes me love you more and more?
How I listen through the hours
For your footsteps at the door.
If, because life is so busy,
I have not renewed my vow,
Let me, on this day of lovers,
Do it most sincerely now.

Good Morning

If I should fail to smile and say "Good morning"
Or miss the lovelight shining in your eyes,
How radiant your face, like new sun rising
Or warmth of summer in the pleasant skies,
Then you may know my soul has had its parting
And I am just a husk behind my face,
When I am not responsive to the blessing,
Which makes this world a lovely dwelling place

Valentine Cookies

With gentle hands she rolled the dough for cookies.
She saw bright eyes above the kitchen table,
And floury noses pressing close to savor
The coming treat and wondered who was able
To not ask please for just a tiny sample
Of spicy, aromatic, chewy dough.
The wood stove warmed our cozy kitchen haven,
Though February fields were white with snow.

She wore a starchy apron, white and lacy,
And cut each cookie out to form a heart.
Love wrapped her family in its golden blanket,
And even baby laughed and took a part.

My memory gems are many, bright and sparkling,
Yet those of deepest fires and brightest shine
Come to me when the world is iced for winter,
And someone bakes warm cookie valentines.

Little Red Valentine

Do you recall our one-room school
When we were full of fun?
And February fourteenth came,
And studying was done?
With squeaking shoes and sidewise glance,
Each walked the center aisle
And dropped his red heart in a box . . .
I was too scared to smile.

A pretty girl would lift the lid
And loudly call the names,
While others sat and hardly breathed
Until their own turns came.
I count the many years since then
And better things I know
Have blest me; yet they're not so dear
As red hearts long ago.

Ice Cream Dawn

All night the snow,
Like frosty feathers from
A darkened sky,
Fell blanketing the earth,
As snowbirds huddled close,
A tight, warm row.
Faint dawn sent rosy streamers
Down the sky,
Smoke curled from chimney tops,
The rasp of shovels met the walk,
A clattering snowplow broke
The chilly silence and
Shook downy flakes from shingled roofs,
All chilly-pearled,
As day crept slowly in,
Awake to find
A fluffy, frosty, fairy,
Ice cream world.

Living Valentines

To see a couple hand-in-hand,
Considerate and sweet,
Lost in a glow that's all their own,
Makes hearts pick up a beat.
What matters if the wind may blow
And bring the winter's chill?
Or if snow drifts the country lanes,
Ice sparkles on the sills?
No frozen earth or icy stream
Can be too deep and wide,
Or bring a gloom into a room
If hearts are warm inside.

Scarlet Friends

I saw two cardinals in the snow,
Upon a fallen tree.
Their scarlet coats looked soft and warm,
Quite beautiful to see.

Though cold winds blew above their crests
And whirled the flakes about,
They perched there in defiance,
To wait the season out.

They come each day for the offerings
That folks strew along the way,
Royal beggars in velvet coats,
Reminders of a balmy day.

They swoop down from the skyway,
And land with easy grace,
King and queen, an ermine throne,
Rubies in a crystal case.

Shirley Sallay

Winter Dawn

Across the morning sky we see,
In flaming colors drawn,
A masterpiece of nature's art,
A frosty morn at dawn.

Lavender and yellow blend
With purple, orange and red;
Flamboyant colors, tier on tier,
Across the heavens spread.

The sun ascends beyond the rim,
To stand in dazzling view,
While colors slowly fade into
A sea of morning dew.

Joy fills the heart and feeds the soul,
When, on a winter morn,
Emblazoned by His handiwork,
Another day is born.

Esther Lee Carter

A Fragile Moment

Morning speaks in silence
As sun and shadow move across the snow
In such a fragile moment
That the heart becomes a chalice to fill with tranquillity
And through the chaos of the day
I need but dip back into the regions of remembrance
To be sustained.

Mona K. Guldswog

The Alchemy of Love

As morning tints suffuse the sky
And turn its gray to gold,
So romance steals into the heart,
Its wonders to unfold.
It touches up life's shabby face
And leaves no drabness there;
With deft and subtle artistry
Love makes the whole world fair.

Some impetus it adds within,
Some precious worth imparts
To common things — all heaven beams
Upon united hearts.
And happy meanings multiply
In joys together found,
For in this bond each finds that love
Still makes the world go round.

B. L. Bruce

February Greetings

All outdoors
Edged in lace,
Twigs and grasses . . .
Beauteous grace.

Sunlight glows
Through snowy birches,
On frosty limb
A bluejay perches.

Thank you, Lord,
For heavenly art.
Your valentine
Has touched my heart.

Adeline Roseberg

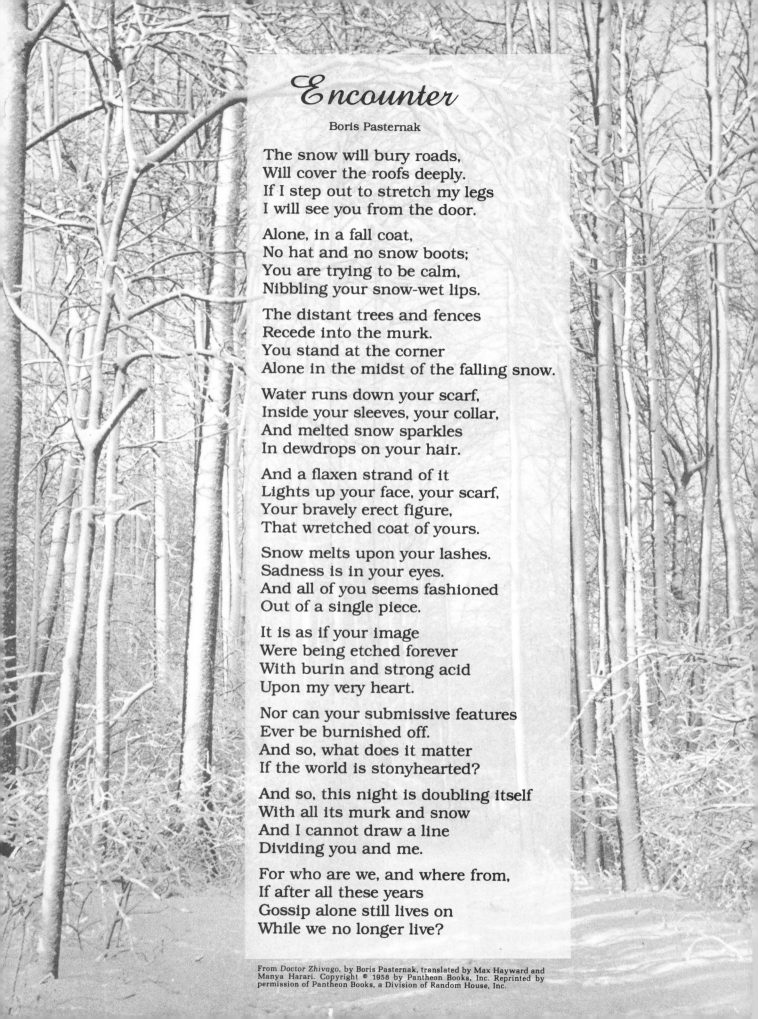

Encounter

Boris Pasternak

The snow will bury roads,
Will cover the roofs deeply.
If I step out to stretch my legs
I will see you from the door.

Alone, in a fall coat,
No hat and no snow boots;
You are trying to be calm,
Nibbling your snow-wet lips.

The distant trees and fences
Recede into the murk.
You stand at the corner
Alone in the midst of the falling snow.

Water runs down your scarf,
Inside your sleeves, your collar,
And melted snow sparkles
In dewdrops on your hair.

And a flaxen strand of it
Lights up your face, your scarf,
Your bravely erect figure,
That wretched coat of yours.

Snow melts upon your lashes.
Sadness is in your eyes.
And all of you seems fashioned
Out of a single piece.

It is as if your image
Were being etched forever
With burin and strong acid
Upon my very heart.

Nor can your submissive features
Ever be burnished off.
And so, what does it matter
If the world is stonyhearted?

And so, this night is doubling itself
With all its murk and snow
And I cannot draw a line
Dividing you and me.

For who are we, and where from,
If after all these years
Gossip alone still lives on
While we no longer live?

From *Doctor Zhivago*, by Boris Pasternak, translated by Max Hayward and
Manya Harari. Copyright © 1958 by Pantheon Books, Inc. Reprinted by
permission of Pantheon Books, a Division of Random House, Inc.

It Was You, God, Who Ordered Roses For the World!

To survive
I must want to survive.
It is beauty that leads me
To desire to continue infinitely.
The beauty of a rose
Is exciting in and of itself,
But when the rose
Has been given
As an experience of love,
Its beauty is irresistible.
It incorporates
The beauty of a human being
As well as its own beauty.
It was You, God,
Who ordered roses for the world!
They are an expression
Of Your love.
Realizing this,
The beauty of a rose
Never fails to lift my heart,
Set it racing,
Awaken my desire
For infinite beauty.
The beauty of God Himself
Flashes forth in each rose.
Yet how many years
Did I look on roses before
Discovering this beauty?

Dr. Leo M. Jones

From *Journey to Survival in a Glorious Manner*,
Copyright 1978 by Leo M. Jones and IRIS, INC.

Beauty Is the Essence Experienced

Developing an eye for beauty
Is a skill necessary for survival.
Why beauty?
It is so frequently
Transitory and fragile.
A rose lasts but a few turns
Of the spiral.

But not the rose bush.
Its life is long compared
To the blossom.
If you are a true rose lover,
Beauty is found in the plant,
Not just the bloom.
The blossom underlies
The entire life of the rose bush,
Even though
It only flashes forth
In the organistic burst
Of the petals and perfume.
Beauty is an expression
Of the essence that is a rose.

To develop an eye for beauty
Is to develop an eye
For the essence,
That is, the essential,
The eternal, the infinite,
The unboundable,
God's grandeur.

Dr. Leo M. Jones

From *Journey to Survival in a Glorious Manner*,
Copyright 1978 by Leo M. Jones and IRIS, INC.

My Valentine

Velta Myrle Allen

Each little word
You say to me
Becomes a pearl
Of memory;
A string of pearls
Ties so secure
True love will
Endlessly endure.

I count each pearl
Upon the string
And deep within
I know and sing
Of tranquil hours,
When you and I
Held the key
To satisfy.

I treasure all these
Shining beads
For they are loving
Thoughts and deeds
That make
A priceless rosary
That you have woven
Just for me.

And yet I wish but for the thing I have.
My bounty is as boundless as the sea,
My love as deep; the more I give to thee,
The more I have, for both are infinite.

Romeo & Juliet Gwen Davenport

The world's best-known lovers of all time, in or out of fiction, met at a masked ball given by the girl's parents to introduce her to another man who was expected to marry her. It was time Juliet Capulet was married, for she was fourteen years old. Her mother, at the same age, had already borne a child.

It was usual to marry young in the Middle Ages, for most lives were brief. A girl's education was complete by the time she had reached her teens, and she was ready for marriage as soon as she was capable of bearing children. Juliet had a handsome suitor, Count Paris, who had asked her parents for her hand. In order that she might meet and approve him, the Capulets had arranged the feast and masquerade party. They had invited everybody in Verona who could be considered anybody—with one exception.

The exception was the Montague family and their young son, Romeo. This family had for generations been carrying on against the Capulets a feud based on an ancient grudge. Their servants and followers often fought in the streets, like rival gangs in modern days. They had been warned by the ruling prince to keep the peace, on penalty of death.

The breach between the families was eventually to be healed, but only at the terrible price of the two young lives of Romeo and Juliet, the "pair of star-crossed lovers" of Shakespeare's romantic tragedy. Verona, the setting, was then a fortified, autonomous state ruled by a great family that kept its power through generation after generation, warding off conquest by neighboring lords. Within the city dwelt lesser noble families, each with its own court and followers. The families of Romeo and Juliet were among these.

For some time, Romeo Montague had been nursing an unrequited passion for a young lady named Rosaline, who had been invited to the Capulet supper. Romeo allowed his friend and kinsman Mercutio to persuade him to "crash the party," as we would say, in order to be where she was. Although he had some misgivings, Romeo was so much infatuated that he donned a mask and joined the dancers in the Capulets' hall.

Juliet stood with her father, receiving their guests. The moment Romeo saw her, he was in love. His feeling for Rosaline had been no more than a rehearsal, so to speak, of falling in love, a testing that had prepared his heart for the greater, all-consuming passion it was now to feel. He did not know who this girl was, but instantly he put his first impression into beautiful poetry:

O, she doth teach the torches to burn bright!
It seems she hangs upon the cheek of night
Like a rich jewel in an Ethiop's ear;
Beauty too rich for use, for earth too dear
. . . Did my heart love till now? Forswear it, sight!
For I ne'er saw true beauty till this night.

Overhearing this, Lady Capulet's nephew, Tybalt, recognized the speaker's voice and knew him for Romeo. Tybalt, a bully, called for his sword and swore to kill the hated Montague on the spot. Juliet's father, however, forbade any fighting in his house, or even a show of inhospitality, saying that he had never heard any ill spoken of this particular young man, and to throw him out would make a scene and spoil the party for the other guests. Romeo was to be allowed to remain for the one evening.

The one evening was time enough to do the mischief. Romeo spoke to Juliet and made it plain to her that he had been smitten by love. Not knowing his identity, she allowed herself to be swept off her feet in turn and fell in love as immediately and thoroughly as he had done. Too late, she learned from her nurse, after Romeo had left, that he was a hated Montague. This nurse, a garrulous and ribald old woman as Shakespeare draws her, had literally nursed Juliet in babyhood and had since remained at her side as a combination maid and companion.

When Juliet learned what had happened, she cried to the nurse:

My only love sprung from my only hate!
Too early seen unknown, and known too late!
Prodigious birth of love it is to me
That I must love a loathèd enemy.

In view of the thunderbolt that had struck them both, it was impossible that either of the lovers should sleep that night. Instead of going home with Mercutio and his friends, Romeo leaped over the wall of the Capulet garden to gaze up at his beloved's window. Juliet, thinking of him to whom she had so impetuously given her heart, wandered out on her balcony to look at the moon and sigh. The love scene that followed, Shakespeare's famous balcony scene, contains some of his most beautiful and oft-quoted lines. It begins with Romeo's words, "He jests at scars that never felt a wound. But soft! what light through yonder window breaks? It is the east, and Juliet is the sun . . ."

Later Juliet says:

'Tis but thy name that is my enemy;
Thou art thyself, though not a Montague.
What's Montague? It is nor hand, nor foot,
Nor arm, nor face, nor any other part
Belonging to a man. O, be some other name!
What's in a name? That which we call a rose
By any other name would smell as sweet. . . .

Romeo lingered beneath the balcony until the night was nearly spent. Before he left, the lovers had agreed they would arrange to marry. Juliet had promised to send her nurse to him for instructions by nine o'clock in the morning, before she left him with the words, "Good-night, good-night! Parting is such sweet sorrow, That I shall say good-night till it be morrow."

Early in the morning, Romeo visited the cell of his friend, Friar Laurence, and persuaded him to perform a secret marriage. Friar Laurence assented only because he thought such an alliance between the houses of Montague and Capulet would surely end the rancor between them and establish peace. After the ceremony, the newlyweds separated, each returning home.

Romeo's friends, meanwhile, had run into Tybalt on the street. The Capulet was out looking for Romeo to challenge him to a duel for having dared invade Capulet territory. Pugnacious as ever, Tybalt ran afoul of Romeo's friend, Mercutio and started a quarrel. Romeo met the two on his way home and did his best to make peace between them, wishing to conciliate the enemy who was now, although Tybalt did not know it, his kinsman by marriage. Mercutio, who could not bear to see Romeo placate the villain, started a fight with Tybalt, in which Romeo intervened. In the fray Mercutio fell mortally wounded, dying with the famous words, "A plague on both your houses!"

Enraged at the death of his best friend, Romeo would no longer turn the other cheek to the murderer. He engaged Tybalt in a duel of vengeance, and Tybalt fell.

continued

Now Romeo, facing the wrath of the Capulets and of the ruling prince, realized he must flee Verona or be killed. "Oh, I am fortune's fool!" he cried. He escaped just before the Capulets discovered Tybalt's body and demanded retribution. The prince, ruler of the city, was at the limit of his patience with this troublesome family feuding and declared categorically that he would put up with it no more. Romeo was to be exiled. If he should ever be found again in Verona, that hour would be his last.

The news of his banishment was brought to Romeo in Friar Laurence's cell, where he had taken refuge. At first he was overcome by despair, but the Friar persuaded him to leave secretly for Mantua and remain there until the families could be reconciled and the prince be persuaded to rescind his edict. Romeo agreed to go before the dawn watch could find him in the city, and he went to spend the night with his secret bride. They became truly husband and wife before Romeo was forced to part from her for he knew not how many months or years.

In the early morning Lady Capulet came to her daughter's room and, finding Juliet in tears, assumed they were shed for the dead Tybalt. The mother announced to her daughter that she was betrothed to Paris, the wedding to take place almost immediately and very quietly, as the household was in mourning. Stunned, Juliet tried every excuse to say she could not and would not marry Paris—every excuse, that is, except the valid one that she was already married. Finally her father harshly ordered her to do his bidding and marry the man he had chosen for her, or go out in the fields to graze, he cared not where, for he would not harbor an undutiful daughter in his house.

The wretched Juliet sought out Friar Laurence, on the pretext of making a confession that she had displeased her father. Casting herself down before him, she threatened to kill herself. But the friar had a plan. If Juliet were brave enough to die, then she must be brave enough to feign death. He offered her a potion that would produce a semblance of death for forty-two hours. She was to drink it on the eve of her wedding to Paris; then instead of being married next morning, she would be carried to the Capulet burial vault to be laid away. Friar Laurence promised that instead of being buried she would be rescued by Romeo and himself, and carried off secretly to Mantua to be with her true husband in exile. He undertook to get word to Romeo of the plot.

Filled with foreboding, Juliet nonetheless took the potion and was found in bed on her wedding day by her parents and nurse, apparently dead. They took her, amid much mourning, to the vault of the Capulet family and there left her. Meanwhile, the friar's messenger failed to get to Mantua and deliver the message to Romeo, so that Romeo's first word of his bride since

their parting was the news of her death. Determined to die beside her rather than live in banishment without her, he bought a vial of poison and went back to Verona and the burial vault.

The grieving Count Paris had come to lay flowers on Juliet's grave when he saw Romeo attempting to pry open the tomb. Paris held Romeo responsible, as Tybalt's murderer, for the grief that had supposedly killed Juliet. Assuming Romeo to have come to do some villainous shame to the dead bodies, he rushed forward, crying, "Stop thy unhallowed toil, vile Montague! Can vengeance be pursued farther than death?" Romeo pleaded with Paris to leave him alone, but Paris apprehended him for a felon and Romeo, now provoked into fury, drew his sword. They fought, and Paris was killed. As he died, he begged to be allowed to lie in death beside Juliet.

Now Romeo opened the tomb to look for the last time on his love, still so strangely beautiful as the bride of Death. In his speech of farewell to life he cried, "Eyes, look your last! Arms, take your last embrace! Here's to my love!" Then he drank the poison and said, "Thus with a kiss I die."

Friar Laurence came hurrying to the vault to arouse Juliet from the trance. He saw the bodies of the two men and, waking the girl, tried to persuade her to come swiftly away with him from that fearful place, saying, "A greater power than we can contradict hath thwarted our intents." He wanted to take her to a refuge in a sisterhood of nuns, but she would not leave Romeo. Snatching up his dagger, before the Friar realized her design, she killed herself and fell dead on Romeo's still-warm body.

When the men of the watch heard the disturbance and came to investigate, they sent immediately for the Montagues and Capulets and for the prince. All of them gathered at the tomb to learn what tragedy their feuding had brought upon them. In their sorrow, the bereaved parents agreed to end the quarreling; it was the only thing they could do now for their dead children.

"All are punished," said the prince:

> A glooming peace this morning with it brings;
> The sun for sorrow, will not show his head.
> Go hence, to have more talk of these sad things;
> Some shall be pardoned, and some punished:
> For never was a story of more woe
> Than this of Juliet and her Romeo.

These are the last words of Shakespeare's great classic drama of tragic love. Among the names of those whom the prince threatened to punish must surely have been that of Friar Laurence, whose ill-conceived attempts to manage things had turned out so badly. The fact that in the end he sincerely regretted his meddling could not put matters right after it was too late.

Mr. Lincoln, President

Alice Leedy Mason

Abraham Lincoln,
Backwoods child,
Born when the States
Were young and wild.
Spent his childhood
In sweet content,
Hardly knew the name
Of the president.

Young A. Lincoln,
Loving son,
Worked through the dusk
Till his chores were done,
Studied in the firelight's
Shadowy glow
Built himself a ferry
'Cross the Ohio.

Captain Lincoln,
Six foot and more,
Served his country
In the Black Hawk War.
First to enlist
When the call came in.
Proved himself
A stalwart leader of men.

Honest Abe Lincoln,
Man of law,
Felt compassion
For the hurt he saw.
Lean of stature,
Quick of wit,
Strong as the roughhewn
Rails he split.

Man of honor,
Firm in strife,
Saw the humor
In his daily life—
Turned to God
For the courage lent—
Mr. Lincoln,
President!

Daily Valentines

Cleo King

How sweet to get a valentine
   Of plain or fancy art,
A rose so pink and violets, too.
   Or satin-covered heart.

But more than beauty or design,
   We prize the words that say
The sender's love comes with the gift
   In quite the warmest way.

We like to know that someone cares,
   That someone wants to do
The kindly deed that makes us feel
   Well loved and happy, too.

So why not give expression then,
   To love for friends so dear,
Not only on one certain day
   But many times a year?

Our valentines may be a smile,
   A cheerful word or two,
A helping hand, a tender glance
   That signals, "I love you."

And if we often take the time
   To give these friendly signs,
The world will soon be brightened by
   Our daily valentines.

North Woods Notebook
Winter, 1930

My husband, Bob, was the youngest of ten children born to Comb and Anna Andersen Bourgeois. The family lived in Park Falls, Wisconsin, when Bob was born on August 20, 1923; during his childhood there were several moves to farms and small towns throughout northern Wisconsin.

Bob's memories of his childhood remain vivid. When he talks about those distant days, the memories come alive; they are echoes of a way of life that has all but disappeared from the American scene.

When I was seven years old, my family moved from Park Falls to a farm in a Chippewa Indian Settlement between Bayfield and Cornucopia, Wisconsin. Dad had lost a leg in a railroad accident while he was working for the Soo Line, and he had to find some way to support our large family. The farm, with its apple orchards and some land for growing fruits and vegetables, seemed like the answer. Dad's pension from his service in the Spanish American War would supplement our earnings from whatever produce we could sell.

Winters were especially hard. The house we lived in had no central heating—we kept warm near the wood stove in the kitchen and the parlor stove in the living room—no electricity, and no running water.

I used to dread getting up at 6 A.M., hopping out of a warm bed onto a freezing floor and dressing in a hurry, knowing that one of my early-morning jobs was to draw water from the well. Before I could leave for school, I also had to carry logs from the woodshed to fill both the woodboxes.

Our well was on a hill about a block from the house. We covered it with boards to keep out dirt, debris, and curious critters. In winter, of course, the water was frozen; before we could lower the buckets and draw water, we had to crack the coating of ice with a long wooden pole. I remember that I was always terrified of falling in.

We filled two buckets each time, because it was easier to carry two than one. No matter how careful we were, some of the water invariably slopped over onto our pants legs, so that by the time we got back to the house we were shivering in frozen trousers. We hung them near the kitchen stove to dry.

It's so simple, nowadays, to turn on a tap and fill a glass with water. But water was a continual problem during those years in the Settlement. Before Ma could do the weekly laundry, we had to haul tubs of water on a sleigh from the well to the house. We also filled wooden tubs with snow, starting the night before washday, and put them on the kitchen stove to melt.

Baths were either a weekly treat or a weekly chore, depending on your place in line. There were at least two baths to a tub, and of course no one liked being second; the water was dirty, and it had cooled down after the first bath. Ma's cook stove had a reservoir that she kept filled with water, and she would add hot water from that or from the ever-present teakettle.

The ordinary business of living took a lot of effort in those years. We were in an isolated rural area, so there was no "running to the store" for food or provisions. Dad killed deer in the winter, and Ma canned the venison. Dad also set snares for rabbits; in the winter, rabbits travel over the same path and beat down the snow, so it's easy to see where they run. Dad made nooses (or snares) out of wire, and he would hang them on a low tree branch over the rabbits' runway. Every morning my brothers and I had to check the snares and bring in the night's catch for Ma to skin, gut, and clean. Since we had no refrigeration, she kept the rabbits in pans on the back porch where they would freeze and keep until spring.

Each winter, we used skis or snowshoes to get to school through the heavy snow. Dad made skis for all of us out of maple or oak boards, and we got our leather snowshoes by trading rabbits or canned goods with the Indians. My brothers and I skied over the deep snow to a one-room schoolhouse that held twenty-two students in all eight grades.

On Saturday nights the schoolhouse became a dance hall, where the adults would square dance and do the Circle Two Step. The "orchestra" was strictly local talent—anyone who could strum a banjo or squeeze an accordion. The ladies brought homemade treats, and those Saturday nights were the shining moments of our long winters.

When we were snowbound, Ma taught us (boys included) how to crochet, knit, and embroider. Sometimes we cut pictures out of an old Montgomery Ward catalog and glued them into homemade scrapbooks. We listened to Dad's favorite program, "Amos 'n' Andy," on a battery-powered radio; when the battery ran down, we had to wait until the next trip into town to have it recharged.

Dad's pension check arrived at the beginning of the month, and my parents would drive into Bayfield to buy staples. They brought home fifty-pound bags of flour, bags of sugar and salt, and huge boxes of Mother's Oats.

Just before the family left Park Falls, Ma had acquired an electric washing machine that was her pride and joy. Even though the house in the Settlement had no electricity, she wasn't about to leave that machine behind when we moved. So she brought it along, and kept it in a pantry off the kitchen.

I'll never forget that washing machine, because it played a part in one of the soundest spankings I ever got in my life.

One winter day I was feeling particularly sorry for myself, and I decided to leave home. I even announced my plans, although nobody seemed shaken at the news.

Before supper, I ran through the orchard out to the road, and slid down into the ditch to hide. I stayed there for quite awhile, sure that my heartbroken parents would come looking for me. They didn't. And as it grew dark, I began to get very cold—not to mention hungry and scared.

So I sneaked back into the house, very quietly, and hid behind Ma's washing machine. I could hear the family talking about me as they devoured Ma's fried chicken, and I felt very smug.

After supper they all put on their coats and boots and went out to look for me. They were gone for what seemed an eternity, and I began to feel very guilty for scaring them so badly. Finally they came home; Ma was crying and sniffling, and Dad was wondering out loud "where in tarnation" I could be.

I appeared from my hiding place, sure that I would be kissed and hugged and provided with a heaping plate of leftovers. I was wrong. Instead, I got a stern lecture from Ma, a spanking from Dad—whose hands were as big as dinner plates—and a one-way ticket to my room.

I never did get dinner that night. I never ran away again, either.

Bea Bourgeois

Winter

As the snow falls gently against my window I give thanks, O Divine Spirit, for the cyle of the seasons and for the ever-changing beauty of the universe. A mantle of purity is spread over the drab earth, and the evergreens bow humbly in their vestments of white. The noises of men cease; a new stillness envelops the world, and Thy voice speaks to me through the elements.

Surely the Power that can create a billion snowflakes, in numberless variety and of perfect symmetrical form, to sparkle for a moment in the sunlight and then vanish, is also mindful of me and the length of my days.

As I look upon this beauty, I think of Thee as the source from which it all comes, and I am drawn closer to Thee. Give me faith to believe that the order which sustains the ever-varying pageantry of nature will also uphold me. Lord of Life, make me quiet long enough to hear Thee speak above the murmur of my desires, the clamor of much speaking, and the confusions of mankind. Breathe into my life the peace and purity of the snow. Amen.

Robert Merrill Bartlett

Even Though the Breeze Blows Chilly

Winter days so brisk and airy,
Snow-white fur on tree and ground,
Oh, so soft the gentle coating,
Beauty beams from all around.

Somehow everything seems purer,
In a place where snow has lain,
And the things which looked unsightly,
Take on brilliance once again.

Children's voices on a hillside,
As they swiftly make their way,
Listen to the joyful laughter,
Happy little hearts at play.

There's tobogganing and skiing,
And there's skating for a sport,
Oh, so many, many pleasures,
Some of every type and sort.

Even though the breeze blows chilly,
Winter's glamor stands alone,
As sunshine on the fluffy snow
Brings a rapture all its own.

Anton J. Stoffle

Winter's Blanket

Winter spread a blanket
Over every hill and glen,
All soft and white and lovely
To thrill our hearts again,
A bit of fun and frolic,
A snowdrift calm and still,
While youngsters' hearts were happy,
As they coasted down the hill.

Winter spread a blanket,
Putting diamonds on the snow,
The world was bright and smiling
As the morning brought a glow,
The air so crisp and frosty,
With the pond all frozen hard,
And a snowman with a high hat
In the nearby neighbor's yard.

Winter brought a beauty
And a magic much more real,
A bit of lovely sparkle
And a happiness ideal,
There were diamonds on the snowflakes
And a smile the world could see.
We thrilled to winter's blanket,
Dressing every naked tree.

Garnett Ann Schultz

Hans Brinker or The Silver Skates

here was an end to grinding, crushing, and sawing for that day. It was a good thing for the millers near Broek. Long before noon they concluded to take in their sails, and go to the race. Everybody would be there. Already the north side of the frozen Y was bordered with eager spectators; the news of the great skating match had traveled far and wide. Men, women, and children in holiday attire were flocking toward the spot. Some wore furs and wintry cloaks or shawls; but many, consulting their feelings rather than the almanac, were dressed as for an October day.

The site selected for the race was a faultless plain of ice near Amsterdam, on that great arm of the Zuyder Zee which Dutchmen, of course, must call the Eye. The townspeople turned out in large numbers. Strangers in the city deemed it a fine chance to see what was to be seen. Many a peasant from the northward had wisely chosen the twentieth as the day for the next city trading. It seemed that everybody, young and old, who had wheels, skates, or feet at command had hastened to the scene. . . .

Where are the racers? All assembled together near the white columns. It is a beautiful sight. Forty boys and girls in picturesque attire darting with electric swiftness in and out among each other, or sailing in pairs and triplets, beckoning, chatting, whispering, in the fullness of youthful glee. . . .

Twenty boys and twenty girls. The latter by this time are standing in front, braced for the start, for they are to have the first "run." Hilda, Rychie, and Katrinka are among them. Two or three bend hastily to give a last pull at their skate straps. It is pretty to see them stamp, to be sure that all is firm. Hilda is speaking pleasantly to a graceful little creature in a red jacket and a new brown petticoat. Why, it is Gretel! What a difference those pretty shoes make, and the skirt, and the new cap. Annie Bouman is there, too. . . .

The race is about to commence. Twenty girls are formed in a line. The music has ceased.

A man, whom we shall call the crier, stands between the columns and the first judges' stand. He reads the rules in a loud voice:

"The girls and boys are to race in turn, until one girl and one boy have beaten twice. They are to start in a line from the united columns, skate to the flagstaff line, turn, and then come back to the starting point, thus making a mile at each run."

A flag is waved from the judges' stand. Madame van Gleck rises in her pavilion. She leans forward with a white handkerchief in her hand. When she drops it, a bugler is to give the signal to start.

The handkerchief is fluttering to the ground! Hark! They are off!

No. Back again. Their line was not true in passing the judges' stand.

The signal is repeated.

Off again. No mistake this time. How fast they go!

The multitude is quiet for an instant, absorbed in eager, breathless watching.

Cheers spring up along the line of spectators. Huzza! Five girls are ahead. Who comes flying back from the boundary mark? We cannot tell. Something red, that is all. There is a blue spot flitting near it, and a dash of yellow nearer still. Spectators at this end of the line strain their eyes and wish that they had taken their post nearer the flagstaff.

The wave of cheers is coming back again. Now we can see. Katrinka is ahead!

She passes the Van Holp pavilion. The next is

continued

Madame van Gleck's. That leaning figure gazing from it is a magnet. Hilda shoots past Katrinka, waving her hand to her mother as she passes. Two others are close now, whizzing on like arrows. What is that flash of red and gray? Hurrah, it is Gretel! She too waves her hand, but toward no gay pavilion. The crowd is cheering, but she hears only her father's voice, "Well done, little Gretel!" Soon Katrinka, with a quick, merry laugh shoots past Hilda. The girl in yellow is gaining now. She passes them all, all except Gretel. The judges lean forward without seeming to lift their eyes from their watches. Cheer after cheer fills the air; the very columns seem rocking. Gretel has passed them. She has won.

"Gretel Brinker, one mile!" shouts the crier.

The judges nod. They write something upon a tablet which each holds in his hand.

While the girls are resting, some crowding eagerly around our frightened little Gretel, some standing aside in high disdain, the boys form in a line.

Mynheer van Gleck drops the handkerchief this time. The buglers give a vigorous blast.

The boys have started!

Halfway already! Did ever you see the like! . . .

A cloud of feathery ice flies from the heels of the skaters as they "bring to" and turn at the flagstaffs.

Something black is coming now, one of the boys: it is all we know. He has touched the *vox humana* stop of the crowd; it fairly roars. Now they come nearer—we can see the red cap. There's Ben—there's Peter—there's Hans!

Hans is ahead! Young Madame van Gend almost crushes the flowers in her hand; she had been quite sure that Peter would be first. Carl Schummel is next, then Ben, and the youth with the red cap. The others are pressing close. A tall figure darts from among them. He passes the red cap, he passes Ben, then Carl. Now it is an even race between him and Hans. Madame van Gend catches her breath.

It is Peter! He is ahead! Hans shoots past him. Hilda's eyes fill with tears; Peter *must* beat. Annie's eyes flash proudly. Gretel gazes with clasped hands; just four strokes more will take her brother to the columns.

He is there! Yes, but so was young Schummel just a second before. At the last instant, Carl, gathering his powers, had whizzed between them and passed the goal.

"Carl Schummel, one mile!" shouts the crier.

Soon Madame van Gleck rises again. The falling handkerchief starts the bugle: and the bugle, using its voice as a bowstring, shoots off twenty girls like so many arrows.

It is a beautiful sight, but one has not long to look; before we can fairly distinguish them they are far in the distance. This time they are close upon one another; it is hard to say as they come speeding back from the flagstaff which will reach the columns first. There are new faces among the foremost—eager, glowing faces, unnoticed before. Katrinka is there, and Hilda, but Gretel and Rychie are in the rear. Gretel is wavering, but when Rychie passes her, she starts forward afresh. Now they are nearly beside Katrinka. Hilda is still in advance, she is almost "home." She has not faltered since that bugle note sent her flying; like an arrow still she is speeding toward the goal. Cheer after cheer rises in the air. Peter is silent, but his eyes shine like stars. "Huzza! Huzza!"

The crier's voice is heard again.

"Hilda van Gleck, one mile!"

A loud murmur of approval runs through the crowd, catching the music in its course, till all seems one sound, with a glad rhythmic throbbing in its depths. When the flag waves, all is still.

Once more the bugle blows a terrific blast. It sends off the boys like chaff before the wind, dark chaff I admit, and in big pieces.

It is whisked around at the flagstaff, driven faster yet by the cheers and shouts along the line. We begin to see what is coming. There are three boys in advance this time, and all abreast—Hans, Peter, and Lambert. Carl soon breaks the ranks, rushing through with a whiff. Fly, Hans, fly, Peter, don't let Carl beat again—Carl the bitter, Carl the insolent! Van Mounen is flagging; but you are strong as ever. Hans and Peter, Peter and Hans; which is foremost? We love them both. We scarcely care which one is the fleeter.

Hilda, Annie, and Gretel seated upon the long crimson bench, can remain quiet no longer. They spring to their feet, so different, and yet one in eagerness. Hilda instantly reseats herself; none shall know how interested she is, none shall know how anxious, how filled with one hope. Shut your eyes then, Hilda, hide your face rippling with joy. Peter has beaten.

"Peter van Holp, one mile!" calls the crier.

The same buzz of excitement as before, while the judges take notes, the same throbbing of music through the din. . . .

The girls are to skate their third mile.

How resolute the little maidens look as they stand in a line! Some are solemn with a sense of responsibility, some wear a smile half bashful, half provoked, but one air of determination pervades them all.

This third mile may decide the race. Still if neither Gretel nor Hilda wins, there is yet a chance among the rest for the silver skates. . . .

The bugle thrills through them again. With quivering eagerness they spring forward, bending, but in perfect balance. Each flashing stroke seems longer than the last.

Now they are skimming off in the distance.

Again the eager straining of eyes, again the shouts and cheering, again the thrill of excitement as, after a few moments, four or five, in advance of the rest, come speeding back, nearer, nearer to the white columns.

Who is first? Not Rychie, Katrinka, Annie, nor Hilda, nor the girl in yellow, but Gretel, Gretel, the fleetest sprite of a girl that ever skated. She was but playing in the earlier races, *now* she is in earnest, or rather something within her has determined to win. That lithe little form makes no effort; but it cannot stop, not until the goal is passed!

In vain the crier lifts his voice; he cannot be heard. He has no news to tell; it is already ringing through the crowd. *Gretel has won the silver skates!*

Like a bird she has flown over the ice, like a bird she looks about her in a timid, startled way. She longs to dart to the sheltered nook where her father and mother stand. But Hans is beside her, the girls are crowding round. Hilda's kind, joyous voice breathes in her ear. From that hour, none will despise her. Goose-girl or not, Gretel stands the acknowledged Queen of the Skaters!

With natural pride Hans turns to see if Peter van Holp is witnessing his sister's triumph. Peter is not looking toward them at all. He is kneeling, bending his troubled face low, and working hastily at his skate strap. Hans is beside him at once.

"Are you in trouble, mynheer?"

"Ah, Hans! that you? Yes, my fun is over. I tried to tighten my strap, to make a new hole, and this botheration of a knife has cut it nearly in two."

"Mynheer," said Hans, at the same time pulling off a skate, "you must use my strap!"

"Not I, indeed, Hans Brinker," cried Peter, looking up, "though I thank you warmly. Go to your post, my friend, the bugle will be sounding in another minute."

"Mynheer," pleaded Hans in a husky voice. "You have called me your friend. Take this strap, quick! There is not an instant to lose. I shall not skate this time. Indeed I am out of practice. Mynheer, you *must* take it"—and Hans blind and deaf to any remonstrance, slipped his strap into Peter's skate and implored him to put it on. . . .

"You are a noble fellow, Hans!" cried Peter yielding at last. He sprang to his post just as the white handkerchief fell to the ground. The bugle sends forth its blast, loud, clear, and ringing.

Off go the boys!. . . .

They are winged Mercuries every one of them. What mad errand are they on? . . .

The chase turns in a cloud of mist. It is coming this way. Who is hunted now? Mercury himself. It is Peter, Peter van Holp! Fly, Peter! Hans is watching you. He is sending all his fleetness, all his strength into your feet. Your mother and sister are pale with eagerness. Hilda is trembling and dares not look up. Fly, Peter; the crowd has not gone deranged, it is only cheering. The pursuers are close upon you! Touch the white column! It beckons; it is reeling before you—it—

"Huzza, Huzza! Peter has won the silver skates!"

"Peter van Holp!" shouted the crier. But who heard him? "Peter van Holp!" shouted a hundred voices, for he was the favorite boy of the place. "Huzza! Huzza!"

Now the music was resolved to be heard. It struck up a lively air, then a tremendous march. The spectators, thinking something new was about to happen, deigned to listen and to look. . . .

Peter and Gretel stand in the center in advance of the other skaters. Madame van Gleck rises majestically. Gretel trembles, but feels that she must look at the beautiful lady. She cannot hear what is said, there is such a buzzing all around her. She is thinking that she ought to try and make a courtesy, such as her mother makes to the meester, when suddenly something so dazzling is placed in her hand that she gives a cry of joy.

Then she ventures to look about her. Peter, too, has something in his hands. "Oh! oh! how spendid!" she cries, and "Oh! how splendid!" is echoed as far as people can see.

Meantime the silver skates are flashing in the sunshine, throwing bright dashes of light upon those two happy faces.

Mevrouw van Gend sends a little messenger with her bouquets—one for Hilda, one for Carl, and others for Peter and Gretel.

At the sight of the flowers the Queen of the Skaters becomes uncontrollable. With a bright stare of gratitude, she gathers skates and bouquet in her apron, hugs them to her bosom, and darts off to search for her father and mother in the scattering crowd.

Mary Mapes Dodge

Fallow Fields

Fallow fields, how still you lie
Beneath the snow and winter sky;

But there's beauty in your calm repose,
Unbroken as the fierce wind blows,

With delicate tracery in snow and sleet,
Or greening field of winter wheat.

Sleep on, dear fields, you need your rest;
Renew your strength from earth's deep breast.

When breaks the spring you'll bloom again
And give rich yield of fruit and grain.

By this we know the cold, bare sod
But waits the touch of a living God.

Anna Vallance

Winter Wonderland

This winter wonderland is mine,
To see and share with you.
Another gift of perfect love,
Another dream come true.

This winter wonderland is formed,
With jewels that shine so bright.
Each snow star has its own design,
Each crystal has its light.

This winter wonderland is filled
With trees that wear a gown,
Made out of dainty webs of snow,
With diamonds on each crown.

This winter wonderland is blessed,
With love that never dies,
Handcrafted by the King of Kings,
Who made the earth and skies.

Patricia Ann Emme

Winter Walk

Come and walk with me, along the snowy ways,
Enjoy the crispy feel, of cold and golden days.
Come and walk with me, beside the icy stream,
Listen to it singing, lightly flinging, winter's theme.
Come and walk with me, around a woodsy bend,
Discover footprints, soft sprints, to a foxes den.
Come and walk with me, to wait the evening fall,
Watch the sun turn pink, slowly sink, this is best of all.

Diane Workman Scott

Skating: Winter's Oldest Sport

Throughout history, people living in northern climates have eagerly anticipated the arrival of winter's peaceful beauty. With the countryside wrapped in blankets of snow and the ponds and rivers stilled by the frigid temperatures, the landscape emerged as an ideal setting for the joys and thrills of ice skating.

Before winter sports became fashionable as an outlet for physical exercise, skating and skiing originated as practical methods of transportation. Skating can be traced to the Neolithic Period when early man used flat pieces of wood tied under each foot to travel over the ice and snow. This technique evolved into more refined skating practices and crude skates made from the shank bones of elk, ox, reindeer, and other animals. These skates were about twelve inches long with a tapered front "prow" and square ends. Holes were drilled into the ends, through which leather thongs were slipped to attach the skates to the feet. The word *skate* has its roots in the German word *schake*, meaning "a shank bone or leg bone." The word *schenkel*, meaning "shank," is used in Holland for a modern steel skate.

Despite the early evidence of skating in Scandinavia, it is not surprising that skating has been practiced in Holland since the Middle Ages as a means of locomotion across the numerous ponds and canals from one village to another. The first iron blade for skates was probably invented in the Netherlands, and by the seventeenth century skating had grown into a national pastime. A typical Dutch skate before the turn of the century had a metal blade with a front "prow" that turned or curled upward. This distinguishing feature enabled the skater to glide safely over rough and cracked ice without catching a tip and taking a nasty spill.

Because of the antics of Dutch seamen at the Great Frost Fair on the Thames River in London in 1683, skating became widely known and very popular among the English people. Ballads of the time described these antics very vividly:

The Rotterdam Dutchman, with fleet-cutting scates,
to pleasure the crowd shows his tricks and his feats;
Who, like a rope dancer (for his sharp steels),
His brains and activity lies in his heels.

The popularity of skating in England spread to Scotland, where in the second half of the eighteenth century, the Edinburgh Skating Club, the first skating club in the world, was founded.

Skating was probably introduced to North America by British officers who were stationed here during the eighteenth century. Colonel Howe, brother of the general of revolutionary fame, was a leading exponent of skating while he resided in Philadelphia. Within a short time Philadelphia became the most important skating center and founded the first skating club in the country. The city also produced the first all-metal skate in 1848, when a man named E.V. Bushnell invented a skate on which both the blade and footplate were made of metal.

In the 1850s a frenzy of ice skating swept our country, due in part to a greater interest in more manly physical exercise. To meet the growing demand for ice skates many companies were founded, such as the Winslow Skate Company in Worcester, Massachusetts, Union Hardware of Torrington, Connecticut, and Barney & Berry of Springfield, Massachusetts. The *New York Ledger* stated in 1862:

"It is said that the rush for skates this season exceeds anything of the kind ever before known in this country. It is supposed that sales will reach a long way up among the millions."

On a good winter's day, as many as fifty thousand skaters crowded the ponds in Central Park, and similar scenes could be found in almost every other city and small town. What a sight it must have been to see young ladies dressed in their finest velvet dresses skating hand-in-hand with gentlemen in long black frock coats, ties, and top hats, while rosy-faced children scurried about the ice.

In the rural areas, most people could not afford the luxury of manufactured skates from the general store, so they had to rely on their own resources and ingenuity to make homemade skates. The town blacksmith would forge steel runners and attach them to bases carved from wood. Heavy and cumbersome in appearance, these skates did provide many hours of enjoyment to some boy or girl out on the "ole pond."

Because of this widespread popularity, skating emerged from a relaxing pastime into a highly competitive sport. Large crowds gathered at competitions to view the beauty and grace of their favorite skaters. Figure skating in the English style was practiced in a rigid manner, as a science requiring a high degree of skill and execution to perfect special intricate forms on the ice. In the manner of good Victorians, these skaters insisted on formal behavior and military-like discipline for their routine.

In the 1860s, Jackson Haines, an American figure skater, revolutionized the skating world by introducing a theatrical flair to his repertoire and winning the American Championship in New York in 1864. Needless to say, his new style shocked English skating circles, but he went on to a triumphal skating tour in Europe and became the first international skating celebrity. He also was the first person to invent a skate specifically suited to his purpose. A steel blade was forged to the toe and heal plate, which was then screwed to the bottom of his skating boot. This skate provided the strength and support needed to execute the difficult jumps, spins, and turns.

Speed skating did not gain the spectator support of figure skating, but it did capture the interest of young men who pumped their strong, muscular legs to reach amazing speeds on the ice. A thorough description of a racing skate is found in an advertisement from the 1897 Sears Roebuck catalog:

"This skate is made under the personal supervision of Mr. Joseph F. Donoghue, world's champion skater, and is made of the highest grade of material, and by first class mechanics. Mahogany tops, hardened steel runners, nickel-plated, russet harness leather straps, nickel tongue buckles. This skate was designed by Mr. Donoghue, and has been used for the past five years in winning all his great races and making his wonderful records, and his success is as much due to the perfection of these skates as to his own skill."

The price of these skates was a hefty $3.05 but they must have been the envy of every kid on the block.

By 1900, many different types of ice skates were on the market. A page in a 1908 Sears Roebuck catalog lists men's hockey skates, "clamp on" figure skates, racing skates, women's club skates with oak-tanned russet leather straps, double-runner children's skates, and related accessories.

In comfort, quality, and performance, the ice skates of today are far superior to those of yesteryear, but the original concept of the skate has changed very little from the first skates with bone runners. What has changed is the popularity and growth of ice hockey, speed skating, and the installation of fine outdoor and indoor facilities for skaters. Even though skates, ice facilities, and skating expertise have grown to new levels of sophistication, the local skating pond, nestled among the trees, will forever warm our hearts and many a cold winter's night with pleasant memories that epitomize all the happiness and joys that are derived from ice skating: winter's oldest sport.

Thomas M. Sersha

An exquisitive invention this,
Worthy of Love's most honeyed kiss—
This art of writing billet-doux
In buds and odors, and bright hues!
In saying all one feels and thinks
In clever daffodils and pinks;
In puns of tulips, and in phrases,
Charming for their truth of daisies!

Leigh Hunt

Flower Language
Carice Williams

Each flower speaks a language
So tender and sincere.
The rose sends out a message
Of love for all to hear.

The daisy shyly whispers,
"I'll never tell on you"
And violets, sweet and dainty,
Repeat, "I'll e'er be true."

Gardenias say, "You're lovely."
Carnations, soft and white,
Speak out, "You're very pretty
And always a delight."

Thus, flowers have a language
And they in turn impart
A bit of love that's hidden
Deep down within the heart.

Statement of ownership, management and circulation (Required by 39 U.S.C., 3685), of IDEALS, published 8 times a year in: Feb.; Mar.; Apr.; June; Aug.; Sept.; Nov.; Dec. at Milwaukee, Wisconsin for September 1980. Publisher, Ideals Publishing Corporation; Editor, James A. Kuse; Managing Editor, Ralph Luedtke; Owner, Harlequin Holdings, Inc., 306 South State Street, Dover, Delaware 19901. The known bondholders, mortgagees, and other security holders owning or holding 1 percent or more of total amount of bonds, mortgages or other securities are: None. Average no. copies each issue during preceding 12 months: Total no. copies printed (Net Press Run) 341,252. Paid circulation 66,508. Mail subscriptions 173,381. Total paid circulation 239,889. Free distribution 1,102. Total distribution 240,991. Single issue published nearest to filing date: Total no. copies printed (Net Press Run) 224,109. Paid circulation 11,239. Other sales 168,013. Free distribution 1,046. Total distribution 180,298. I certify that the statements made by me above are correct and complete. Donald A. Gottschalk, President.

COLOR ART AND PHOTO CREDITS
(in order of appearance)

Front and back cover, Colour Library International (USA) Limited; inside front and back cover, Alpha Photo Associates; Old-fashioned valentines, Gerald Koser; Swan vase, Colour Library International (USA) Limited; Cozy room, Gerald Koser; Family at fireplace, Colour Library International (USA) Limited; Fruit fare, Gerald Koser; Covered bridge, Fred Sieb; Gift of Love, Colour Library International (USA) Limited; Yellow house, Colour Library International (USA) Limited; Ferns, Gerald Koser; Nostalgic bouquet, Colour Library International (USA) Limited; Chickadee, Fred Sieb; Skiers, Tom Stack; Old wagon, Colour Library International (USA) Limited; WINTER KISS, Ed Gifford; Winter forest, Ed Cooper; Valentine gems, Fred Sieb; Hearts and flowers, Colour Library International (USA) Limited; Valentine tea, Fred Sieb; Church, Fred Sieb; Children in snow, Freelance Photographers Guild; Hans Brinker, Dennis Hockerman; Winter cornfield, Ken Dequaine; WINTER MORNING, Currier & Ives, Three Lions, Inc.; Sunset, Josef Muench; Keepsake, Fred Sieb.

ACKNOWLEDGMENTS

WINTER by Robert Merrill Bartlett. From Boys Prayers, the Ascending Trail by Robert Merrill Bartlett, published by Association Press. Reprinted with permission. WINTER WHITE by Grace E. Easley. Previously published in The Family Album, 1979. FOREST-FINDINGS IN BLUE SHADOWS by Rhea Smith Meek. Previously published in Pasque Petals, January 1956. Used with permission. THE BASKET SOCIAL by Grace Sellers. From Good Old Days, July 1973. Used with permission. Our sincere thanks to the following author whose address we were unable to locate: Esther Lee Carter for WINTER DAWN.

Welcome Spring . . .

Enjoy the splendor and beauty of awakening nature in prose, poetry and photography in our colorful Easter issue of Ideals.

Visit Oberammergau, Germany, the site of a Passion Play; learn of flower legends that have ''blossomed'' around Easter; revel in the natural beauty of a lagoon inhabited by wild geese; and treasure the writing of our featured poet, Margaret Rorke.

So, welcome Spring with an Ideals subscription, for yourself or as a gift. Enter a refreshing world of timeless beauty that will enhance your reading pleasure all year long!